AUG - - 2022

D1709246

Celebrating
KWANZAA

By Seth Lynch and
Carol Gnojewski

Cavendish
Square

Published in 2023 by Cavendish Square Publishing, LLC
29 E. 21st Street New York, NY 10010

Website: cavendishsq.com

This publication represents the opinions and views of the author based on their personal experience, knowledge, and research. The information in this book serves as a general guide only. The author and publisher have used their best efforts in preparing this book and disclaim liability rising directly or indirectly from the use and application of this book.

Disclaimer: Portions of this book originally appeared in the book *Kwanzaa: Seven Days of African-American Pride* by Carol Gnojewski. All new material in this book authored by Seth Lynch.

All websites were available and accurate when this book was sent to press.

Library of Congress Cataloging-in-Publication Data

Names: Lynch, Seth, author. | Gnojewski, Carol, author.
Title: Celebrating Kwanzaa / Seth Lynch, Carol Gnojewski.
Description: New York : Cavendish Square Publishing, 2023. | Series:
Celebrating our holidays | Includes index.
Identifiers: LCCN 2021040020 | ISBN 9781502664785 (library binding) | ISBN
9781502664761 (paperback) | ISBN 9781502664778 (set) | ISBN
9781502664792 (ebook)
Subjects: LCSH: Kwanzaa–Juvenile literature. | African Americans–Social
life and customs–Juvenile literature.
Classification: LCC GT4403 .L96 2023 | DDC 394.2612–dc23
LC record available at https://lccn.loc.gov/2021040020

Editor: Kristen Nelson
Copyeditor: Jill Keppeler
Designer: Deanna Paternostro

The photographs in this book are used by permission and through the courtesy of: Cover, pp. 1, 11 MIND AND I/Shutterstock.com; back cover, pp. 3, 5, 6, 9, 10, 15, 18, 21, 23, 25, 26, 28, 29, 20, 31, 32 N.D.Vector/Shutterstock.com; p. 4 Ailisa/Shutterstock.com; p. 6 Prokhorovich/Shutterstock.com; pp. 7, 23 (main) PenWin/Shutterstock.com; p. 8 Rawpixel.com/Shutterstock.com; p. 12 anon_tae/Shutterstock.com; p. 14 catwalker/Shutterstock.com; p. 17 Danilo Marocchi/Shutterstock.com; p. 18 bestjeroen/Shutterstock.com; p. 20 Timothy R. Nichols/Shutterstock.com; p. 22 Image Source Trading Ltd/Shutterstock.com; p. 23 (sidebar) Nejah/Shutterstock.com; p. 24 Caratti E Poletto adv/Shutterstock.com; p. 26 bilha golan/Shutterstock.com; p. 27 5D Media/Shutterstock.com; p. 28 (hot glue gun) XIE WENHUI/Shutterstock.com; p. 28 (beads) Nataliia Spivak/Shutterstock.com; p. 28 (scissors) IB Photography/Shutterstock.com.

Some of the images in this book illustrate individuals who are models. The depictions do not imply actual situations or events.

CPSIA compliance information: Batch #CSCSQ23: For further information contact Cavendish Square Publishing LLC, New York, New York, at 1-877-980-4450.

Printed in the United States of America

Find us on

CONTENTS

In the African language of Swahili, *kwanza* means "first."

CHAPTER ONE
Come Together for Kwanzaa

Holidays are about bringing people together. Family and friends often gather for a big meal on Thanksgiving. They may share their faith on Christmas, Hanukkah, and Diwali. Kwanzaa, a holiday created by and for Black Americans, is also about gathering with family. What's more, it's about uniting with other members of the Black community.

Kwanzaa is based on seven **principles** that aid those celebrating in looking at their past and **heritage**. They think about who they are now and use this knowledge to plan for a bright future. The holiday's founder, Maulana Karenga, said he believes that the message of Kwanzaa is universal: "Any message that is good for a particular people speaks not just to that people. It speaks to the world."

Kwanzaa is special in many ways. Perhaps the most obvious one is that this holiday is less than 60 years old! Many well-known holidays have hundreds of years of history. Kwanzaa's history is still being

HOLIDAY OR HOLY DAY?

Many of the winter holidays celebrated in the United States have a connection to a particular faith. The word "holiday" comes from Old English words that mean "holy day." Today, we use the word to mean religious holy days as well as days on which people are off work or celebrating something. Kwanzaa is a holiday, but it isn't tied to any particular faith and is celebrated by people who have different religious beliefs.

Kwanzaa is a nonreligious, or secular, holiday. It is tied to the culture of Black Americans but not to any particular faith.

The candles are labeled, from left to right: Unity, Self-Determination, Collective Work and Responsibility, Cooperative Economics, Purpose, Creativity, Faith.

Kwanzaa shares some practices, like lighting special candles, with other holidays.

written. It began during a difficult time for Black Americans and connects with Black people today as they continue their fight for equality.

Kwanzaa grew out of the protests and activism of the 1960s.

CHAPTER TWO
KWANZAA'S ROOTS

Kwanzaa was created in 1966 by a teacher and activist named Dr. Maulana Karenga. He wanted Black Americans to have a holiday that honors Black culture and **identity**, much of which has roots in Africa. He felt there were strong traditions, or practices, there that had been lost in the United States. Karenga didn't want Black Americans to forget their past as enslaved people, their unequal treatment, or how far they had come. He believed they should take control of their lives and their communities.

STARTS IN CALIFORNIA

Karenga lived in Los Angeles, California. There, an event that became known as the Watts rebellion (or Watts **riots**) occurred in 1965 in a Los Angeles neighborhood. The people who lived there were mostly Black. Two men were pulled over by police, and an argument started. The argument grew to include others from the neighborhood, and protests and then riots broke out. The riots and fights with police continued for six days. Homes and businesses were damaged. More than 30 people died, and many more were injured. This was the backdrop against which Karenga created Kwanzaa.

The United States in the 1960s

Black Americans' history in the United States is full of **discrimination** and poor treatment. By 1966, the civil rights movement was well underway. This was a time when Black Americans organized to fight for equal rights as citizens of the United States. In 1964 and 1965, the government passed laws that made discrimination illegal in voting, hiring for jobs, and being in public places. However, Black Americans still fight against discrimination today.

Karenga wanted to help after these events occured. He wanted to lift up Black culture and honor it through his work. He founded a group to help those in the neighborhood rebuild. The group wanted to start a holiday that connected Black Americans with their heritage and gave them pride in it.

African Roots

Karenga based Kwanzaa partly on harvest festivals celebrated all over Africa, including festivals of the Ashanti and Zulu peoples. The name of the holiday comes from the Swahili phrase *matunda ya kwanza*. Swahili is a language spoken in many parts of Africa. The phrase means "first fruits." In Africa, "first fruits" refer to crops of food that people gather or harvest at the end of the growing season.

Karenga planned the holiday to take place from December 26 to January 1. In some African cultures, these days are called "the time when the edges of the year meet."

A first-fruits harvest festival honors the land and all that grows each year. It brings people together to celebrate shared bonds of family and life.

People who celebrate Christmas, Hanukkah, or any other winter holidays are also free to celebrate Kwanzaa if they like.

Karenga also wanted to have Kwanzaa be an alternative holiday for some Black Americans to celebrate instead of Christmas. He said he wanted to "give Blacks an opportunity to celebrate themselves and their history, rather than simply [copy] the practice of the [main] society," which meant that of white Americans. Kwanzaa wouldn't be based in any one faith and could be celebrated by anyone who chose to do so.

PLANNING THE HOLIDAY

Creating Kwanzaa was a way for Karenga to help Black Americans understand their rich history and culture. He wanted them to see their lives from an African point of view.

In his own life, Karenga decided that "the first step forward is a step backward to Africa and African roots." He studied African history. He traveled to many African countries and talked to people there. He learned how they lived and what was important in their lives. The wisdom he gathered became the Nguzo Saba.

The Nguzo Saba is a list of seven principles, or teachings, that are celebrated during Kwanzaa. There are seven principles for the seven days of Kwanzaa, each represented by a word in Swahili:

Day 1 *Umoja*: unity
Day 2 *Kujichagulia*: self-determination
Day 3 *Ujima*: collective work and responsibility
Day 4 *Ujamaa*: cooperative economics
Day 5 *Nia*: purpose
Day 6 *Kuumba*: creativity
Day 7 *Imani*: faith

Karenga wrote down what he learned, what the principles of Kwanzaa are, and how it would be celebrated so others could follow the guidelines.

In 1997, the U.S. Post Office issued the first stamp honoring Kwanzaa.

CHAPTER THREE
Early Celebrations

Karenga and his friends held the first Kwanzaa celebration in 1966 in California. It wasn't well known outside of certain groups for many years. During the late 1970s, though, it began to become more of a part of Black American culture.

Magazines Spread the Word

In 1979, *Essence* magazine published the first article all about Kwanzaa. *Jet* and *Ebony* magazines also wrote about the holiday. These magazines were very popular among Black Americans. They likely introduced Kwanzaa to many people in the United States.

By the late 1980s, people began to teach about Kwanzaa in some schools. Then, in the 1990s, President Bill Clinton was the first U.S. president to acknowledge the holiday, stating, "The principles of Kwanzaa—unity, self-determination, collective work and responsibility, cooperative economics, purpose, creativity, and faith—ring true not only for African Americans, but also for all Americans."

The Celebration, Day by Day

Kwanzaa lasts for one week. Each day, people light candles in a special candleholder called a kinara. From the early celebrations of Kwanzaa to today, the structure of the holiday hasn't changed much.

December 26

This is the first day of Kwanzaa. The black candle in the kinara is lit. *"Habari Gani* (Hah-BAH-ree GAH-nee)?"* an adult will ask. "What's the news?" The response is *"Umoja!"* This means unity. Families, friends, and neighbors come together for umoja night. In some communities, they meet at town centers, churches, or halls. Everyone lights a candle. They make a wish for the New Year.

December 27

People light a black and a red candle in the kinara. The day is about *kujichagulia,* or self-determination. Families may talk about what it means to be Black or have African heritage. Everyone is encouraged to think about who they are and what they can do to find out more about themselves and their history.

December 28

Those celebrating light a black candle, a red candle, and a green candle in the kinara. This day's theme is *ujima,* or collective work and responsibility. Together, families do household chores such as cleaning out a workroom or planning a spring garden. They may visit older relatives and help them clean or cook a meal.

December 29

This day's candles include one black candle, two red candles, and one green candle. The principle discussed is *ujamaa,* or cooperative economics. Money and wealth are the focus of this day. Families may save money all year to make a big purchase everyone will use.

Big cities such as Chicago, Illinois, hold ujamaa holiday markets. These are flea markets and arts and crafts fairs similar to the open-air markets

The Makola Market in Ghana is found right in the center of the city of Accra.

found in African cities. African clothing, musical instruments, art, food, and handmade items are sold there.

African Style

During Kwanzaa, many Black people wear African clothing and hairstyles. This style can vary from place to place. People may wear beads and other jewelry or braid them into hair and clothes. Boys may wear dashikis (dah-SHEE-kees), or long, loose shirts. They also may wear flat, round hats that are called kufis (KOO-fees). Some women wrap their heads with scarves called geles (GAY-lays). In Northern Africa, some women wear veils that cover their hair and face. Men who live there may wear a headpiece called a turban.

Braided hairstyles are common among Black people worldwide. Tight rows of braids are often called cornrows. Dreadlocks are another African hairstyle. They form over time when sections of hair are rolled up or braided.

December 30

People light one black candle, two red candles, and two green candles in the kinara. To *"Habari Gani?"* people respond *"Nia!"* This means purpose. A roll call to the **ancestors** is a Kwanzaa **ceremony** that honors personal and historical heroes. An adult will begin by naming an important African or Black American. Family members who have passed away are also named.

December 31

Those celebrating light one black candle, three red candles, and two green candles in the kinara. Creativity, or *kuumba*, is the principle of the day.

A *karuma* is a harvest feast. There are no set Kwanzaa menus, so families cook their own favorite recipes. Southern foods, such as greens, sweet potatoes, and fried chicken, are often served. Creole dishes, such as a stew called jambalaya, and African foods, such as plantains, might also be present. Hoppin' John, a southern dish made with black-eyed peas, is said to bring luck in the New Year.

Before the meal, an elder will pour water from the unity cup into a bowl of lettuce or greens. The elder will spill the water four times—one for each of the four directions: north, south, east, and west. Then, they will speak to the ancestors and drink from the cup. The cup is passed around the table, and everyone takes a drink. This ceremony is called *tambiko* (tahm-BEE-koh).

January 1

All of the candles in the kinara are lit. To *"Habari Gani?"* the final response is *"Imani!"* This means faith.

The last day of Kwanzaa is a day of meditation. When you meditate, you are quiet and thoughtful. You think about your life and how you can make it better. Some families think about the changes in their lives over the past year. There might have been births, weddings, and funerals. People have moved away from or entered into the family. All these joyful and sad events are remembered.

The seven symbols of Kwanzaa are often seen together in a display in people's homes and community centers.

CHAPTER FOUR
Symbols of Kwanzaa

In the celebration of Kwanzaa, the number seven is important. This is based on the seven principles set forth by Karenga. The holiday is seven days long and has seven major **symbols**.

Seven Symbols

The seven Kwanzaa symbols are the: *mkeka* (m-KAY-kah), or mat; *mazao* (mah-SAH-o), or fruits and vegetables; *kikombe cha umoja* (kee-KOM-bay cha oo-MO-jah), or unity cup; *muhindi* (moo-HEEN-dee), or corn; kinara (kee-NAH-rah), or candleholder; *mishumaa saba* (MEE-shoo-MAH-ah SAH-bah), or seven candles; and *zawadi* (sah-WAH-dee), or gifts.

The mat, or mkeka, is often made of straw or cloth that comes from Africa. The mkeka represents the **foundation** of heritage, personal history, and traditions upon which a person's life is built. It's also a literal foundation for the other symbols in a Kwanzaa display. Mazao—the fruits and vegetables—are often put into a basket or bowl on a Kwanzaa display. These represent, or stand for, the harvest festivals upon which the holiday is based. Because African families worked together in their fields, these harvest festivals were more than just parties. They meant coming together to celebrate the work and bounty of the harvest. So, mazao also symbolize work and a job well done.

Corn, muhindi, is a separate Kwanzaa symbol from the harvest. It is a grain that grows in South Africa. Each corn kernel is a seed that

Each family's kinara may be unique, but they all represent the same thing: African ancestors.

can be planted to grow more corn. In Kwanzaa symbolism, children are like seeds. They are the future. One ear of corn is collected for each child in the family. People who do not have children add an ear of corn to the display too. In many places in Africa, everyone in the community raises the children.

The kikombe cha umoja, or unity cup, is an important part of the holiday of Kwanzaa. Family members drink together from this cup. This is done as an offering to the ancestors. Many unity cups are made of wood or metals such as silver or pewter.

The kinara is the name for the candleholder at the center of many daily Kwanzaa traditions. It is put in the center of a Kwanzaa display. Kinaras are often made of wood, but they can be any shape as long as they hold seven candles. The kinara itself represents ancestors who are no longer on Earth but who can help protect their family from evil and danger.

Other symbols—the candles, or mishumaa saba—are placed in the kinara. There are three red candles, three green candles, and a black candle. The black candle is placed in the center. It stands for Africans and Black Americans. Red candles are placed on the left. They stand for the struggles of daily living. The green candles go on the right. Their green color stands for future hopes.

The black candle is lit first. Red and green candles are added to those lit on alternating nights. Red candles are lit before green ones. This is to show that hard work and struggle lead to a better future. As each day of Kwanzaa passes, another candle is lit until all the candles are lit on the final night.

Family gifts—zawadi—are the final Kwanzaa symbol. They can be homemade. They can be useful, such as books. People often give gifts made in Africa or bought from a store owned by Black Americans.

Kente Cloth

Kente is a type of cloth often from the country of Ghana. Kings and queens of the Ashanti people had their own patterns of kente cloth made as far back as the 12th century. It's woven with bright colors and has come to symbolize the past and beliefs of the culture of Ghana. Today, shirts, pants, hats, dresses, and stoles made of kente are worn during Kwanzaa.

The colors and designs woven into kente cloth have special meanings.

The Kwanzaa Flag

The black, red, and green *bendera* (ban-DAY-rah) is the Kwanzaa flag. It is based on a flag created by Marcus Garvey, a Black leader. The colors of the flag have a special meaning. Like the candles used in the kinara, black stands for the people. Red stands for struggle. Green stands for future hopes. The flag is hung with the black stripe on top to show that people come first.

During Kwanzaa, communities and cities may raise a Kwanzaa flag. Families may hang it outside their homes to show their pride in celebrating the holiday. Outward displays like this are a way to connect with the original intention of Kwanzaa: to bring together Black Americans to honor a common heritage.

Hanging the bendera is one way to show others you celebrate Kwanzaa.

Today, Kwanzaa celebrations continue to connect Black Americans with each other.

CHAPTER FIVE

Kwanzaa Today

Though Kwanzaa was created in the United States for Black Americans, it's now celebrated by people of African **descent** all over the world. People in the countries of the Caribbean embraced Kwanzaa. Like the United States, these countries were places where enslavers took many enslaved Africans in the past.

Today, Kwanzaa is a part of Black culture in the United States. Black Americans who celebrate it may have direct ancestral ties to Africa, or they may have a different heritage. According to Karenga, one need not be fully African—or even Black—to enjoy Kwanzaa. The holiday also brings together people of all different faiths and backgrounds. Nonetheless, some reports say the number of people celebrating Kwanzaa has been decreasing.

Pulling Together

Kwanzaa was created during a time in which some Black Americans were questioning their identity as a group. They wanted to band together and create traditions that were all their own. Since then, colleges have started more Black studies classes and programs. The internet connects people with each other and their heritage more than ever before. Some experts think Kwanzaa participation has declined simply because the ideas of the holiday are being taught and shared more than they were in the 1960s and 1970s.

Commercial Kwanzaa

The number of people who celebrated Kwanzaa reached its peak in the late 1980s and early 1990s. Major stores began to make decorations, including kinaras, to sell to people observing the holiday. In 1996, it was reported that the Kwanzaa market was worth about $500 million. The holiday became more and more **commercial**, which turned off people who wanted to stay true to the original principles and feeling of the holiday.

Though Kwanzaa isn't as popular as it once was, there are still decorations and cards to buy during the holiday season.

Still, recent events in the United States have recalled the civil rights movement to many people's minds. Black Americans are standing together to protest discrimination, particularly their treatment by police. A renewal in celebrating the unity of Black people at Kwanzaa may not be far away.

Make It Your Own

Kwanzaa is about bringing together communities and families, but not every day of Kwanzaa needs to be as busy as is described in this book. Many people have a simple candle ceremony every evening in which they

The history of Kwanzaa is alive at every Kwanzaa celebration today.

gather with friends or family members. They light the proper candles and talk about the principle of the day. They may read a poem or passage from a Black writer. The unity cup may be passed around for everyone to drink from. How you want to celebrate Kwanzaa is up to you—and in choosing how you want to celebrate, you are upholding the very foundation of the holiday!

HOLIDAY HOW-TO

Make A Decorative Unity Cup

You Will Need:

large plastic or wooden cup
small beads in many colors
nylon thread
scissors
hot glue gun with glue sticks

Make your Kwanzaa celebration all the merrier with this colorful cup! Ask an adult to help you when using the glue gun.

DIRECTIONS:

1. Place your beads in a bowl. Cut a long length of thread, and make a knot at one end.

2. Begin stringing beads onto the thread. Consider making a pattern of colors inspired by Kwanzaa in black, red, and green.

3. Try wrapping the beaded thread around the cup. When it can wrap around 5 times, trim the thread, leaving about 3 inches (7.6 centimeters) after the last bead. Knot the thread to keep the beads in place.

4. With the help of an adult, warm up a hot glue gun. You will be making lines of glue around the cup. Squeeze just a few inches of glue on at a time and press the beaded thread into the glue.

5. Once the length of the beaded thread is glued down, cut off any extra thread. Allow it to cool and dry.

GLOSSARY

ancestor: A relative who lived long before you.

ceremony: An event to honor or celebrate something.

commercial: Having to do with the buying and selling of goods and services.

culture: The customs, beliefs, and ways of life of a group of people.

descent: Having to do with the people in your family who lived before you.

discrimination: Unfairly treating people unequally because of their race, beliefs, or something else.

foundation: An idea that gives support for something.

heritage: Traditions or property from earlier generations of ancestors.

identity: Who a person is.

principle: A value that guides people's actions.

riot: A public disturbance during which people may become violent.

symbol: An object that represents or stands for an idea or thought.

FIND OUT MORE

Books

Bullard, Lisa. *My Family Celebrates Kwanzaa*. Minneapolis, MN: Lerner Publications, 2019.

McAllister, Angela. *A Year Full of Stories*. New York, NY: Frances Lincoln Children's Books, 2016.

Otto, Carolyn. *Celebrate Kwanzaa*. Washington, D.C.: National Geographic, 2017.

Websites

Holidays for Kids: Kwanzaa
www.ducksters.com/holidays/kwanzaa.php
Review Kwanzaa and other December holidays on the Ducksters website.

Kwanzaa
kids.nationalgeographic.com/celebrations/article/kwanzaa
Learn even more about Kwanzaa on the *National Geographic Kids* site.

Kwanzaa Crafts
www.activityvillage.co.uk/kwanzaa-crafts
Find more Kwanzaa crafts here!

INDEX